I BELIEVE!

Original Collective Poems

Gayle Phillips-Roberson

COPYRIGHT

TABLE OF CONTENTS

Copyright

Dedication

Acknowledgements

1
Sunrise
2
The Shepherd
3
Call Him
4
He Is For You
5
My Destiny At the Cross
7
In His Name
8
His Grace
9
The Day the Lord Had Made
11
The Coming of the Lord
13
The Lord's Prisoner
14
Thank You, Holy Spirit

15

Storms

17

Sunshine

18

Salvation

19

Clouds

20

He's Working It Out

21

It's Just the Beginning

22

Eternity

23

Joyful! Joyful!

24

Fruit of the Spirit

25

Praises of All Creation

26

Faith

27

For Me

28

The Face of God

29

Psalms

31

Goodness and Mercy

32

Rainbows

33

Just to Touch Him

34

Lift Me

35

In His Presence

36

Our Sins

37

When We Sing

39

Solitude

41

My Faith

42

Sunset

Read the Bible 3 Passages A Day For 365 Days

DEDICATION

"DEREK"

A Father
A Brother
A Friend
A Son
He worked hard
He endured
And now his work is done.
His mortal vessel
No longer holds
That which was created to be free
His immortal spirit
To now live
For all eternity.
His smile that only his loved ones knew
We'll forever carry in our hearts,
And that smile will always remind us,
That in a short time
We'll all be together
And never part.
The Father knows best
For those who don't understand
Even though his spirit has passed on,
Know that there's peace and rest
And the Master forever holds him in His Hand.

ACKNOWLEDGMENTS

My gratitude of love and thanks to everyone who inspired me to keep writing. God bless you all.

Also, at the end of the book, there's a 365-days reading Bible reading schedule that I hope will increase your faith. I encourage you to read it.

And to all who read this book – Enjoy, and Continue to believe.

I Believe

SUNRISE

Sunrise is the first light of life,
As that new life begins so fresh, so new,
That life holds a treasure chest of hopes
and dreams
And God's many unending promises so
true.

The dew from early sunrise
Inspires a new day of His amazing Grace.
It glistens on each tiny leaf,
As His blessings shines on each adoring
face.

Each sunrise brings new beginnings,
As each day our lives He charts.
He promises if we would but delight in
Him,
With each sunrise He'll give us the desires
of our hearts.

THE SHEPHERD

He is the Good Shepherd
My Shepherd
I find peace
Solitude
In the green pastures and still waters
Of my soul.
He restores me,
My path is that of the upright
For I choose to do His Will
I find comfort as my loved ones sleep.
There is no fear
In the evil that men do.
As He stretch forth
His staff of protection.
My enemies are round about me,
Yet He's fed me,
Sheltered me among them.
And I am protected,
I am safe.
I am anointed with His favor
And His blessings overflow.
There's no loneliness
Only goodness and mercy
Forever and forever
Wherever I go.

CALL HIM

God has a phone number?
It's Jeremiah 33:3.
It says if you would but call Him,
There are great and mighty things He
would show thee.

First, He would show you His Majesty,
To be praised both here and now,
And then as you begin to praise,
As you, every knee would bend and head
bow.

Next, He would show His healing grace,
And no longer will you live in pain.
All it would take is just a call to Him,
For you to be restored once again.

Another of His great wonders
Is to turn your mourning into joy.
That is why He sent His Son, our Lord,
To bring peace with life and not to destroy.

His wonders are truly amazing,
And there are more wonders He wants to
show thee.
So if you would like to know more,
Just call Him at Jeremiah 33:3.

HE IS FOR YOU

*When your enemies are both far and near
As they try to hold back that which is true.
Just stay strong, hold on
Because God is forever for you.*

*Some say your past is who you are
And you will never be able to break free
But the Lord said when He went to the
Cross,
The old is now new because of Calvary.*

*The odds seem to mount higher against you
As you push forward toward your destiny,
The enemy will continue to try break your
will
But he'll fail because God is for both you
and me.*

MY DESTINY AT THE CROSS

My destiny was sealed at the Cross
All those hours He hung there for me,
The stripes, the torture, the beatings, the
pain
The endless hours of agony.

For my destiny to be sealed at the Cross,
He had to be denied not one time, not two,
but three

As they led Him away to His fate on the hill
To that hill we call Calvary.

My destiny was sealed at the Cross
As He whispered through the pain "I
thirst".
Why didn't He just raise His head and
come down,
Because, He had to make old things new
first.

For my destiny to be sealed at the Cross,
He had to forgive those who were taking
His life.
So He asked the Father to forgive what
they do,
Even though He knew it would not end His
strife.

For my destiny to be sealed at the Cross
He had to hang between a robber and a
thief
One sealed his fate as he refused to accept
Him
The other would be in paradise, because of
his belief.

For my destiny to be sealed at the Cross,
He had to cry out to the Father and ask
why,
The pain made Him feel as if He had been
so forsaken,
Even though for my destiny to be sealed He
had to die.

As my destiny was sealed at the Cross,
He looked to his mother and brother and
said to behold
He then said it is now finished
Because it was all predestined, all foretold.

So now my destiny has been sealed at the
Cross,
Because He crossed over from this earth to
glory,
And He sits at the right hand of the Father
always,
And my destiny is with Him through all
eternity.

IN HIS NAME

As you reach for the stars high above,
For the stars are the goals you wish to achieve,
You can go farther than the stars, even the
moon,
For in His Name you asked because you have
faith and believe.

The dreams that at one time seemed
impossible,
Are one by one now coming true.
There is no doubt His favor is on each of those
dreams,
Because in His Name you asked Him to bless
you.

HIS GRACE

I woke this morning
Felt Him touch my face,
His voice touched my heart and said,
"I wake you by my Grace."

As I stepped from my bed
Ready to begin this day's Christian race,
I felt my feet, my hands and body move,
And He said "You move it all by my Grace."

I went about my workday
And prayed each task would fall into place,
Each time it did, I gave Him thanks,
And He said "It was all done by My Grace."

I'm sad to say, I somewhat strayed
From His Will for me for this day
Please forgive me Lord, bring me back to
You
And He did by His saving Grace.

The sun sets, it's day's end
Each of His blessings I thankfully embrace,
Just as I close my eyes I felt His touch
And He tells me, "Your peaceful rest will be
by my Grace."

THE DAY THE LORD HAD MADE

Lord, I know You've planned my day
From my waking up to my lying down.
And everything in between that time,
You've filled with Your Mercy abound.

You've filled it with Your forgiveness,
For the times you knew I would fall,
You would then pick me up, renew my
strength

And say, "If you need Me, all you need do
is call."

You lovingly directed my path today,
Because there were times I felt somewhat
lost,
But You whispered gently in my ear and
said,
"If you need Me, just seek Me at the Cross.

You also watched over my loved ones
today,
And you blessed them as You did me.
You also kept them from all hurt and harm,
And for that, I also thank thee.

There were times I just needed to be still
And let Your Will be done.
I hope I did this in Jesus' Name,
For in doing so, today's victories were won.

It's day's end now and as I reflect,
And pray Lord I gave You my best.
I thank You and ask You to keep watch
over me,
As I lay me down to rest.

THE COMING OF THE LORD

I had a dream of the day the Lord returned
I was caught up with those who lived and
who slept,
He stretched out His arms and welcomed us
all
And said, "You're here because your faith in
Me you kept."

I asked "Lord, is it really you?"
"Yes He said, Oh yes it's me,
The Mansion that I prepared for you,
Is now ready for you to dwell for all eternity".

"Look around and see your loved ones are
here
Who were caught up just as were you,
And as tears began to swell in my eyes
I looked around and saw it was all true.

The first I saw was my dear mother,
Whose sweet smile I remembered from years
past.
As she opened her arms for our first
embrace,
She said, "my daughter, you're finally home
at last".

"Oh, Mama," I have so much to say"
"I know", she said, and so have I."
But for now, let's just enjoy this time,
And we did, as I continued to cry.

The next one I saw was my beloved son
Whom for years I mourned every day.
He then flashed that precious smile that I
missed,
As he happily walked my way.

I felt your pain through each tear that you
shed,
And I prayed your mourning would cease
I wanted to tell you I'm living my life after
death
And with the Lord, my soul is now at peace.
I heard each prayer that you prayed for me
And I knew your love for me would live on,
So I always kept watch over you and other
loved ones,
Because their prayers for me were just as
strong.

I then saw other loved ones and friends
Who were also caught up with our Dear Lord.
Each smiled and welcomed me home also
We then gave thanks to the Father who was
true to His Word.

His sacrifice took the sting out of death
As He also conquered the grave
And all those who believe forever will live
And be caught up with Him and be saved.

THE LORD'S PRISONER

I am a prisoner of the Lord
He holds my heart for eternity
I've surrendered all I have to Him
After He surrendered all on Calvary.

I pray Lord, "Take me as I am,
For I'm Yours from this day hence.
I gladly give my heart and soul to You,
And as a prisoner of your love, I hope it's a
life sentence.

To some, prison only means death and
despair,
No hope of joy or peace,
But to be a prisoner of our dear Lord,
Means a life and love that will never cease.

THANK YOU, HOLY SPIRIT

Holy Spirit, did I thank You today,
For all truth and knowledge you did show.
Did I thank You for the many special ways,
You let Your presence be known.

You touched my spirit and showed me how
To speak the truth in His name.
You also showed me if I would believe,
In Him I would find peace and not shame.

Holy Spirit, You brought comfort to me,
In my many times of grief.
Every time You dried each tear that I shed,
You brought me such blessed relief.

I hope I heard You as You spoke to me,
When You told me to go here and not there.
And I hope I heard You when You also said,
"Like the Father and Son, I do care."

Holy Spirit I need you more and more,
As these perilous times increase.
For I know as long as You walk with me,
In You, my fears I can release.

So, as I go to my knees in prayer tonight,
I thank the Father for His love,
I thank You, Holy Spirit, also,
For Your truth and Divine guidance from
above.

STORMS

The storms of my life seem to rage on and
on,
At times I see no relief in sight.
I know I cannot hold them back
At least not under my own might.

So, I look to Heaven then drop to my knees
And pray, "Lord, the tempest is tossing me
to and fro."
I need Your strength, Your calming peace
And to tell these storms they must go".

I know I brought on some of these storms
Each time I kept You out of my life,
And some I even knew in my heart
Would take me through darkness and not
Your Light.

And when You told me to trust You
With the big as well as the small,
I thought I could make do at the time,
And I really didn't need You at all.

But these storms now grow more and more
The waves are pounding without cease,
No matter where I turn right now,
The tempest rages and there's no release.

Lord, I know not which way to turn,
Cause these storms continue to follow me,
No matter how far I try to run,
These storms will not let me be.

So I now do what I should have at first
That's pray these storms obey Your Will
And I ask you Lord to command these
storms,
By telling them
"Peace, be still."

SUNSHINE

Some days there's no sunshine
Only the tears that seem to endlessly flow
As the dark clouds of despair loom heavily
You seek that ray of sunshine to finally
show.

The sunshine is His promise
That will show through after the rain
His promise is to turn the dark to light
And to bring the sunshine to your life
again.

As you feel the sunshine breaking the dark
clouds,
And feel His promise begin to lift you above
your woes,
And as you look, you see just a glimmer of
hope
As that ray of sunshine begins to show.

SALVATION

I've given my life to the Lord
And the angels in Heaven rejoice
For their joy of my salvation
Makes them shout with a resounding voice.

With my salvation comes freedom
To sing, to dance, to shout.
To know that by His blood I'm redeemed
And to no longer have reason to doubt.

This salvation is so amazing
So fulfilling, so divine
Because this salvation now gives me the
right to say
Yes, Jesus loves me, Yes, Jesus is mine.

CLOUDS

Those clouds that drift so lazily by
Are just Heaven's Angels
Watching over you and I.

HE'S WORKING IT OUT

Heavy burdens
Full of doubt
Even before we ask
He's working it out.

Heart is broken
Dreams seem in doubt
If He instilled in you those dreams,
Then He'll work it out.

He's faithful to His word,
He said just don't doubt,
Just stay strong in your faith,
Cause right now He's working it out.

Burdens lifted
No more reason to doubt
Because He's a faithful God,
He's worked it all out.

IT'S JUST THE BEGINNING

It's just the beginning
And not the end
When you received His gift of salvation,
And He's washed away all your sins.

Before the beginning of time
He was predestined to come,
To intercede for our transgressions
With the shedding of His blood.

This new life is a beginning
That strips away all our shame,
And it gives us the kind of joy and peace
We can only receive in His Name.

So turn from the old
And embrace the new,
Because this is a new beginning,
Through salvation that's freely given to
you.

ETERNITY

Eternity, glorious eternity
Always and forever
No more pain
No more tears
Only length of years
Peace of the Spirit
Peace of the soul,
To dwell in an eternity
Of love, always love.
Streets of gold,
There's no end of the rainbow
To forever worship Him
In spirit and truth.
He's prepared a mansion
For all who believe
With the promise of His return
Always and forever
With Him,
To live in
Eternity,
Glorious eternity.

JOYFUL! JOYFUL!

Joyful! Joyful! Oh joyful!
All the earth shouts, "Oh joyful!"
As I worship Him,
Oh joyful!
I sing songs of praise,
Of joy.
For I am made in His Image;
Oh how joyful!
I am His,
He is mine,
My loving Shepherd;
Joyful! Joyful!
Thanksgiving,
Praise.
I offer Him.
What a joyful thing.
His goodness,
Oh, how joyful!
His love,
How joyous!
The joy of His faithfulness
Goes on and on;
From generation to generation;
All shall sing
Joyful! Joyful! Oh, how joyful!

FRUIT OF THE SPIRIT

The fruit of the Spirit
Paul encourages us to embrace,
This fruit we receive from the Lord
By His Promise and amazing Grace.

The first fruit of His Spirit is Love,
For which the Lord gives so abundantly,
For there is nothing as strong on this earth and
beyond
As His love for both you and me.

Long suffering is just a test of your faith,
When life's journey seems too hard to endure
It will keep you on your knees for strength
And will remind you God's love is assured.

The Meekness and Gentleness of the Spirit
Means you will inherit the Kingdom above,
These fruits do not make you weak,
But gives you strength to show your brother
God's love.
Temperance, Joy, Goodness and Peace
Are fruits that the Lord says we need walk in
and live ,
For if you live by these fruits of His Spirit,
You'll receive victory through the Savior,
Who, all good things to you will give.

This fruit is built on your Faith
A faith that means you are free,
For if you live them in your daily walk
You will daily walk in victory.

PRAISES OF ALL CREATION

The waters of the earth
As they move to and fro,
Give honor to the Father,
Through its strength of abundant flow.

The mountains give salute
To His glory and majesty,
As they stand in awe and touch the tip of
Heaven
And seem to say we worship Thee.

The sun praises by day,
The moon and stars by night.
They all shine on His splendor
And radiate on His righteous might.

The beasts of the field,
The fowl of the air,
They too praise the name of Jehovah God,
As they cover this earth for e're and e're.

His greatest creation
He said "I'll create in the image of Me"
Was the creation of the first man,
Who would give Him the ultimate praise and
glory.

The creation of this world
He created in six days,
Was to build His Kingdom here on earth
And for all creation to worship and give Him
praise.

FAITH

Faith does not confuse your mind,
But makes everything so clear.

When you want to touch the stars,
Faith takes you there and beyond.

When you want to say, "That's it, no more,
Faith tells you, "Don't stop, because today is
your day."

When all you hear are words of
discouragement,
Faith tells you, "You can do all things through
Christ which strengthens you."

When what you you've believed, you no longer
believe,
Faith will give you faith in your belief once
more.

Faith is not too hard to obtain,
And as long as you have faith, there will never
be loss, but gain.

Faith gives you courage to try just one more
time,
Even after you failed over and over again.

Faith does not limit your thinking,
But helps you think thoughts you never knew
you could think.

People say to dream the impossible dream,
With Faith, nothing is impossible.

FOR ME

For me He lived
For me He died
For me He suffered
And promised me life on the other side.

For me He gave hope
For me He gave peace,
For me He gave love
And promised that His love would never
cease.

THE FACE OF GOD

Is that fleecy cloud that just drifted by.
The first smile of a sunrise as it kisses the
sky.
The radiant hues of a rainbow's splendor,
That brightens the sky and goes on forever.

So, I ponder these wonders
That make me think of Grace.
Because as I look at them,
I realize I see God's Face.

PSALMS

Psalms of the Bible are poetry in song
As we give the Father our total praise
These Psalms sing of forgiveness and hope
Which you'll receive through His unending
Grace.

There are Psalms of His mercy
Of His forgiveness and relief
Psalms of pleas for help
And for provision as we strengthen our belief.

King David sang for protection from his enemy
Who pursued him both day and night
Psalms 51 he prayed for God's mercy
For his transgression of taking a life.

He then sang Psalms of thanksgiving
For victory over his enemies far and near
He then danced to the God of Israel
Who if you pray to Him will always hear.

There are Psalms of His protection from the evil
one
Who can befall us all by night or day,
He promises to be our very present help,
In times of trouble that may come our way.

Psalms sings He is the light of our life
As we receive His promise of salvation,
And as we sing a joyful noise unto Him,
His promise will endure from generation to
generation.

Psalms sings of the God of Jacob
And we sing of His goodness and love,
And as we sing praises to him through these
Psalms,
He will return his goodness and mercy from
above.

GOODNESS AND MERCY

I thought I walked alone,
Each day the Lord let me see.
But His word has faithfully promised,
Goodness and Mercy shall always follow me.

With each step that I took
I would often feel somewhat lonely,
But when I looked to my left and then to my
right,
I realized Goodness and Mercy was following
me.

The Goodness of His Spirit
Made me repent of all my sins,
His Mercy is His forgiveness
That showed my heart I could begin again.

His Goodness and Mercy endures forever,
For they are fruit of the spirit we should
obtain,
They are blessings He gives us so freely
As we freely in His Name do claim.

The earth is full of His goodness,
His Mercy endures through all time and
beyond,
Because forever Goodness and Mercy will
follow me,
And I know I will never walk alone.

RAINBOWS

*That glorious rainbow stretching across the
Heavens,
Whose brilliant colors of yellow, orange,
green and blue.
God sent as a ray of hope,
And as a reminder that His Word is forever
true.*

*The rainbow means all is not lost,
For only a while the rain will fall,
Then the likeness of His Glory will appear,
In the form of His rainbow to shine on us
all.*

*Continue to look for the rainbow,
When the storms of life arise and seem to
remain.
Always remember what He promised after
the storm,
If you look up, you'll see the rainbow has
appeared once again.*

JUST TO TOUCH HIM

If I could but touch Him,
Just touch the hem of His robe,
That touch of faith would restore within,
And that which was broken, would then be
made whole.

His touch is like a warm embrace,
Like that of a soothing balm.
It heals and reassures a wounded heart,
And restores it with an everlasting peace
and calm.

All it takes is just one touch from the
Master,
And He will heal my spirit, my heart, my
soul.
For if I can just touch the hem of His robe,
That touch of faith will then make me
whole.

LIFT ME

Lord lift me above my cares
Above my earthly troubles and woes
Lord lift me above all that is not of You,
To that place where all blessings flow.

Lift me to where I can see Your face
Where I can see no other but You alone.
Lord lift me to where You speak favor to
me,
And You tell me all my sins have been
atoned.

Lord lift me to where Your love abounds
And there's an abundance of Grace in Your
Name.
Lord lift me, just lift me, just lift me high,
For the higher I'm lifted, the more of You I
can claim.

IN HIS PRESENCE

I delight in His presence
As I happily sit at His feet
The communion of our spirits
Is so amazing, is so sweet.

I find joy in His presence
My faith is renewed as He speaks.
He promises "I am a faithful God,
And I will strengthen you where you are
weak."
As I delight in His presence
In His hand He gently takes mine.
And reassures that if I would only delight
in Him,
On me His presence will forever shine.

OUR SINS

Our sins are ever before us
They grip our spirit in darkness and shame
Under this mortal flesh of weakness
We know it's wrong, but there we place the
blame.

We see the wrong committed by others daily
Yet, we do nothing but sit and complain
We shake our heads in judgment
And wag our fingers to show our disdain.

We see the strong overwhelm the weak,
Our children are helpless to endure
The old pray for release from this life
For the promise of Heaven that's assured.

So where does the sin really lie?
In the one who sins or who does nothing to
avail?
It would seem the sin lies in both,
For to God, sin is death, and none shall prevail.

But fear not, hope reigns eternal,
And that death can change to life.
If we would but accept Him as Lord and Savior
We shall be saved by the blood of His stripes.

WHEN WE SING

The beat touches my spirit
That makes my head nod amen
The sistah next to me
Rises, sways, claps her hands
The Spirit has touched
Something deep within
All sing
All clap
What does it mean?
When we sing?
Isn't our prayers enough?
Our Tithes?
Our Amens?
So what does it mean?
When we sing?
When our worship turns to song
The tambourine,
The drum,
The harp

The voices that blend in harmony
When we take our worship higher
By singing,
What does it mean?
In the Temple
David bared all
Through his worship,
He danced and sang his psalms of praise.
God smiles as our voices rise
For He knows to Him we sing,
Our voices grow louder

Outstretched hands,
Again He smiles
Because for Him we sing.
Now I know what it means
When we sing.
For to pray,
To clap,
To give,
To sing,
Means,
Total Praise.

SOLITUDE

In my solitude
There is quiet.
In my solitude,
I connect.
As I look up to the Heavens,
I wonder how far it stretches.
I know God is Infinite,
Did He create the Heavens the same way?
How far will He allow us to see?
To touch?
To experience?
To understand?

In my solitude
I come before His presence.
I listen.
For in my solitude
He speaks.
His words surround my heart.
He says, "I hear you, do you hear Me?
Be still and know that I AM."

So, in my solitude I am still.
I listen.
He speaks.
I praise.
He gives.
I receive.
He blesses.
I give thanks,
And I say,
"Thank you, I AM,
For the gift of Solitude."

MY FAITH

The Hand that holds mine, I cannot see,
Yet, I'm certain that Hand
Is guiding and protecting me.

My faith does not blind me
But makes me see so clear,
The dreams of my youth
Are now so evidently near.

My faith is Hope;
Hope encourages,
Encouragement strengthens me.
My strength inspires me;
Inspiration releases my Faith,
And when my Faith is released,
I am hopeful, encouraged, strengthened
and inspired.

SUNSET

Sunset begins the twilight of life,
When by His Grace, hopes and dreams
have been fulfilled,
It's the time when we think of our Heavenly
Home,
And we do not fear Sunset because it's part
of His Will.

As we reflect on our life's trials and
victories,
And His multitude of blessings that flowed,
We give Him all the praise and glory.
For blessings seen and those unknown.

Now as the Sunset of life draws near
And we know without doubt He never left
us alone.
We now wait to hear our Heavenly Father
say,
"My good and faithful servant, well done."

Read the Bible 3 Passages A Day For 365 Days

❖ **Day 1** - Luke 5:27-39; Genesis 1:1-2:25; Psalm 1

❖ **Day 2** - Luke 6:1-26; Genesis 3-5; Psalm 2

❖ **Day 3** - Luke 6:27-49; Genesis 6:1-7:24; Psalm 3

❖ **Day 4** - Luke 7:1-17; Genesis 8-10; Psalm 4

❖ **Day 5** - Luke 7:18-50; Genesis 11; Psalm 5

❖ **Day 6** - Luke 8:1-25; Genesis 12; Psalm 6

❖ **Day 7** - Luke 8:26-56; Genesis 13:1-14:24; Psalm 7

❖ **Day 8** - Luke 9:1-27; Genesis 15; Psalm 8

❖ **Day 9** - Luke 9:28-62; Genesis 16; Psalm 9

❖ **Day 10** - Luke 10:1-20; Genesis 17; Psalm 10

❖ **Day 11** - Luke 10:21-42; Genesis 18; Psalm 11

❖ **Day 12** - Luke 11:1-28; Genesis 19; Psalm 12

- ❖ **Day 13** - Luke 11:29-54; Genesis 20; Psalm 13

- ❖ **Day 14** - Luke 12:1-31; Genesis 21; Psalm 14

- ❖ **Day 15** - Luke 12:32-59; Genesis 22; Psalm 15

- ❖ **Day 16** - Luke 13:1-17; Genesis 23; Psalm 16

- ❖ **Day 17** - Luke 13:18-35; Genesis 24; Psalm 17

- ❖ **Day 18** - Luke 14:1-24; Genesis 25; Psalm 18

- ❖ **Day 19** - Luke 14:25-35; Genesis 26; Psalm 19

- ❖ **Day 20** - Luke 15; Genesis 27:1-45; Psalm 20

- ❖ **Day 21** - Luke 16; Genesis 27:46-28:22; Psalm 21

- ❖ **Day 22** - Luke 17; Genesis 29:1-30; Psalm 22

- ❖ **Day 23** - Luke 18:1-17; Genesis 29:31-30:43; Psalm 23

- ❖ **Day 24** - Luke 18:18-43; Genesis 31; Psalm 24

- ❖ **Day 25** - Luke 19:1-27; Genesis 32-33; Psalm 25

- ❖ **Day 26** - Luke 19:28-48; Genesis 34; Psalm 26

- ❖ **Day 27** - Luke 20:1-26; Genesis 35:1-36:43; Psalm 27

- ❖ **Day 28** - Luke 20:27-47; Genesis 37; Psalm 28

- ❖ **Day 29** - Luke 21; Genesis 38; Psalm 29

- ❖ **Day 30** - Luke 22:1-38; Genesis 39; Psalm 30

- ❖ **Day 31** - Luke 22:39-71; Genesis 40; Psalm 31

- ❖ **Day 32** - Luke 23:1-25; Genesis 41; Psalm 32

- ❖ **Day 33** - Luke 23:26-56; Genesis 42; Psalm 33

- ❖ **Day 34** - Luke 24:1-12; Genesis 43; Psalm 34

- ❖ **Day 35** - Luke 24:13-53; Genesis 44; Psalm 35

- ❖ **Day 36** - Hebrews 1; Genesis 45:1-46:27; Psalm 36

- ❖ **Day 37** - Hebrews 2; Genesis 46:28-47:31; Psalm 37

- ❖ **Day 38** - Hebrews 3:1-4:13; Genesis 48; Psalm 38

❖ **Day 39** - Hebrews 4:14-6:12;
Genesis 49:1-50:26; Psalm 39

❖ **Day 40** - Hebrews 6:13-20;
Exodus 1:1-2:25; Psalm 40

❖ **Day 41** - Hebrews 7; Exodus 3:1-
4:31; Psalm 41

❖ **Day 42** - Hebrews 8; Exodus 5:1-
6:27; Proverbs 1

❖ **Day 43** - Hebrews 9:1-22; Exodus
6:28-8:32; Proverbs 2

❖ **Day 44** - Hebrews 9:23-10:18;
Exodus 9:1-10:29; Proverbs 3

❖ **Day 45** - Hebrews 10:19-39;
Exodus 11:1-12:51; Proverbs 4

❖ **Day 46** - Hebrews 11:1-22;
Exodus 13:1-14:31; Proverbs 5

❖ **Day 47** - Hebrews 11:23-40;
Exodus 15; Proverbs 6:1-7:5

❖ **Day 48** - Hebrews 12; Exodus
16:1-17:16; Proverbs 7:6-27

❖ **Day 49** - Hebrews 13; Exodus
18:1-19:25; Proverbs 8

❖ **Day 50** - Matthew 1; Exodus 20:1-
21:36; Proverbs 9

❖ **Day 51** - Matthew 2; Exodus 22:1-
23:33; Proverbs 10

❖ **Day 52** - Matthew 3; Exodus 24; Proverbs 11

❖ **Day 53** - Matthew 4; Exodus 25-27; Proverbs 12

❖ **Day 54** - Matthew 5:1-20; Exodus 28:1-29:46; Proverbs 13

❖ **Day 55** - Matthew 5:21-48; Exodus 30-32; Proverbs 14

❖ **Day 56** - Matthew 6:1-18; Exodus 33:1-34:35; Proverbs 15

❖ **Day 57** - Matthew 6:19-34; Exodus 35:1-36:38; Proverbs 16

❖ **Day 58** - Matthew 7; Exodus 37:1-38:31; Proverbs 17

❖ **Day 59** - Matthew 8:1-13; Exodus 39:1-40:38; Proverbs 18

❖ **Day 60** - Matthew 8:14-34; Leviticus 1-2; Proverbs 19

❖ **Day 61** - Matthew 9:1-17; Leviticus 3-4; Proverbs 20

❖ **Day 62** - Matthew 9:18-38; Leviticus 5-6; Proverbs 21

❖ **Day 63** - Matthew 10:1-25; Leviticus 7-8; Proverbs 22

❖ **Day 64** - Matthew 10:26-42; Leviticus 9-10; Proverbs 23

❖ **Day 65** - Matthew 11:1-19; Leviticus 11-12; Proverbs 24

❖ **Day 66** - Matthew 11:20-30; Leviticus 13; Proverbs 25

❖ **Day 67** - Matthew 12:1-21; Leviticus 14; Proverbs 26

❖ **Day 68** - Matthew 12:22-50; Leviticus 15-16; Proverbs 27

❖ **Day 69** - Matthew 13:1-23; Leviticus 17-18; Proverbs 28

❖ **Day 70** - Matthew 13:24-58; Leviticus 19; Proverbs 29

❖ **Day 71** - Matthew 14:1-21; Leviticus 20-21; Proverbs 30

❖ **Day 72** - Matthew 14:22-36; Leviticus 22-23; Proverbs 31

❖ **Day 73** - Matthew 15:1-20; Leviticus 24-25; Ecclesiastes 1:1-11

❖ **Day 74** - Matthew 15:21-39; Leviticus 26-27; Ecclesiastes 1:12-2:26

❖ **Day 75** - Matthew 16; Numbers 1-2; Ecclesiastes 3:1-15

❖ **Day 76** - Matthew 17; Numbers 3-4; Ecclesiastes 3:16-4:16

❖ **Day 77** - Matthew 18:1-20;
Numbers 5-6; Ecclesiastes 5

❖ **Day 78** - Matthew 18:21-35;
Numbers 7-8; Ecclesiastes 6

❖ **Day 79** - Matthew 19:1-15;
Numbers 9-10; Ecclesiastes 7

❖ **Day 80** - Matthew 19:16-30;
Numbers 11-12; Ecclesiastes 8

❖ **Day 81** - Matthew 20:1-16;
Numbers 13-14; Ecclesiastes 9:1-
12

❖ **Day 82** - Matthew 20:17-34;
Numbers 15-16; Ecclesiastes 9:13-
10:20

❖ **Day 83** - Matthew 21:1-27;
Numbers 17-18; Ecclesiastes 11:1-
8

❖ **Day 84** - Matthew 21:28-46;
Numbers 19-20; Ecclesiastes 11:9-
12:14

❖ **Day 85** - Matthew 22:1-22;
Numbers 21; Song of Solomon 1:1-
2:7

❖ **Day 86** - Matthew 22:23-46;
Numbers 22:1-40; Song of
Solomon 2:8-3:5

❖ **Day 87** - Matthew 23:1-12; Numbers 22:41-23:26; Song of Solomon 3:6-5:1

❖ **Day 88** - Matthew 23:13-39; Numbers 23:27-24:25; Song of Solomon 5:2-6:3

❖ **Day 89** - Matthew 24:1-31; Numbers 25-27; Song of Solomon 6:4-8:4

❖ **Day 90** - Matthew 24:32-51; Numbers 28-29; Song of Solomon 8:5-14

❖ **Day 91** - Matthew 25:1-30; Numbers 30-31; Job 1

❖ **Day 92** - Matthew 25; 31-46; Numbers 32-34; Job 2

❖ **Day 93** - Matthew 26:1-25; Numbers 35-36; Job 3

❖ **Day 94** - Matthew 26:26-46; Deuteronomy 1-2; Job 4

❖ **Day 95** - Matthew 26:47-75; Deuteronomy 3-4; Job 5

❖ **Day 96** - Matthew 27:1-31; Deuteronomy 5-6; Job 6

❖ **Day 97** - Matthew 27:32-66; Deuteronomy 7-8; Job 7

* **Day 98** - Matthew 28; Deuteronomy 9-10; Job 8

* **Day 99** - Acts 1; Deuteronomy 11-12; Job 9

* **Day 100** - Acts 2:1-13; Deuteronomy 13-14; Job 10

* **Day 101** - Acts 2:14-47; Deuteronomy 15-16; Job 11

* **Day 102** - Acts 3; Deuteronomy 17-18; Job 12

* **Day 103** - Acts 4:1-22; Deuteronomy 19-20; Job 13

* **Day 104** - Acts 4:23-37; Deuteronomy 21-22; Job 14

* **Day 105** - Acts 5:1-16; Deuteronomy 23-24; Job 15

* **Day 106** - Acts 5:17-42; Deuteronomy 25-27; Job 16

* **Day 107** - Acts 6; Deuteronomy 28; Job 17

* **Day 108** - Acts 7:1-22; Deuteronomy 29-30; Job 18

* **Day 109** - Acts 7:23-8:1a; Deuteronomy 31-32; Job 19

* **Day 110** - Acts 8:1b-25; Deuteronomy 33-34; Job 20

- ❖ **Day 111** - Acts 8:26-40; Joshua 1-2; Job 21

- ❖ **Day 112** - Acts 9:1-25; Joshua 3:1-5:1; Job 22

- ❖ **Day 113** - Acts 9:26-43; Joshua 5:2-6:27; Job 23

- ❖ **Day 114** - Acts 10:1-33; Joshua 7-8; Job 24

- ❖ **Day 115** - Acts 10:34-48; Joshua 9-10; Job 25

- ❖ **Day 116** - Acts 11:1-18; Joshua 11-12; Job 26

- ❖ **Day 117** - Acts 11:19-30; Joshua 13-14; Job 27

- ❖ **Day 118** - Acts 12; Joshua 15-17; Job 28

- ❖ **Day 119** - Acts 13:1-25; Joshua 18-19; Job 29

- ❖ **Day 120** - Acts 13:26-52; Joshua 20-21; Job 30

- ❖ **Day 121** - Acts 14; Joshua 22; Job 31

- ❖ **Day 122** - Acts 15:1-21; Joshua 23-24; Job 32

- ❖ **Day 123** - Acts 15:22-41; Judges 1; Job 33

* **Day 124** - Acts 16:1-15; Judges 2-3; Job 34

* **Day 125** - Acts 16:16-40; Judges 4-5; Job 35

* **Day 126** - Acts 17:1-15; Judges 6; Job 36

* **Day 127** - Acts 17:16-34; Judges 7-8; Job 37

* **Day 128** - Acts 18; Judges 9; Job 38

* **Day 129** - Acts 19:1-20; Judges 10:1-11:33; Job 39

* **Day 130** - Acts 19:21-41; Judges 11:34-12:15; Job 40

* **Day 131** - Acts 20:1-16; Judges 13; Job 41

* **Day 132** - Acts 20:17-34; Judges 14-15; Job 42

* **Day 133** - Acts 21:1-36; Judges 16; Psalm 42

* **Day 134** - Acts 21:37-22:29; Judges 17-18; Psalm 43

* **Day 135** - Acts 22:30-23:22; Judges 19; Psalm 44

* **Day 136** - Acts 23:23-24:9; Judges 20; Psalm 45

❖ **Day 137** - Acts 24:10-27; Judges 21; Psalm 46

❖ **Day 138** - Acts 25; Ruth 1-2; Psalm 47

❖ **Day 139** - Acts 26:1-18; Ruth 3-4; Psalm 48

❖ **Day 140** - Acts 26:19-32; 1 Samuel 1:1-2:10; Psalm 49

❖ **Day 141** - Acts 27:1-12; 1 Samuel 2:11-36; Psalm 50

❖ **Day 142** - Acts 27:13-44; 1 Samuel 3; Psalm 51

❖ **Day 143** - Acts 28:1-16; 1 Samuel 4-5; Psalm 52

❖ **Day 144** - Acts 28:17-31; 1 Samuel 6-7; Psalm 53

❖ **Day 145** - Romans 1:1-15; 1 Samuel 8; Psalm 54

❖ **Day 146** - Romans 1:16-32; 1 Samuel 9:1-10:16; Psalm 55

❖ **Day 147** - Romans 2:1-3:8; 1 Samuel 10:17-11:15; Psalm 56

❖ **Day 148** - Romans 3:9-31; 1 Samuel 12; Psalm 57

❖ **Day 149** - Romans 4; 1 Samuel 13; Psalm 58

❖ **Day 150** - Romans 5; 1 Samuel 14; Psalm 59

❖ **Day 151** - Romans 6; 1 Samuel 15; Psalm 60

❖ **Day 152** - Romans 7; 1 Samuel 16; Psalm 61

❖ **Day 153** - Romans 8; 1 Samuel 17:1-54; Psalm 62

❖ **Day 154** - Romans 9:1-29; 1 Samuel 17:55-18:30; Psalm 63

❖ **Day 155** - Romans 9:30-10:21; 1 Samuel 19; Psalm 64

❖ **Day 156** - Romans 11:1-24; 1 Samuel 20; Psalm 65

❖ **Day 157** - Romans 11:25-36; 1 Samuel 21-22; Psalm 66

❖ **Day 158** - Romans 12; 1 Samuel 23-24; Psalm 67

❖ **Day 159** - Romans 13; 1 Samuel 25; Psalm 68

❖ **Day 160** - Romans 14; 1 Samuel 26; Psalm 69

❖ **Day 161** - Romans 15:1-13; 1 Samuel 27-28; Psalm 70

❖ **Day 162** - Romans 15:14-33; 1 Samuel 29-31; Psalm 71

- ❖ **Day 163** - Romans 16; 2 Samuel 1; Psalm 72
- ❖ **Day 164** - Mark 1:1-20; 2 Samuel 2:1-3:1; Daniel 1
- ❖ **Day 165** - Mark 1:21-45; 2 Samuel 3:2-39; Daniel 2:1-23
- ❖ **Day 166** - Mark 2; 2 Samuel 4-5; Daniel 2:24-49
- ❖ **Day 167** - Mark 3:1-19; 2 Samuel 6; Daniel 3
- ❖ **Day 168** - Mark 3:20-35; 2 Samuel 7-8; Daniel 4
- ❖ **Day 169** - Mark 4:1-20; 2 Samuel 9-10; Daniel 5
- ❖ **Day 170** - Mark 4:21-41; 2 Samuel 11-12; Daniel 6
- ❖ **Day 171** - Mark 5:1-20; 2 Samuel 13; Daniel 7
- ❖ **Day 172** - Mark 5:21-43; 2 Samuel 14; Daniel 8
- ❖ **Day 173** - Mark 6:1-29; 2 Samuel 15; Daniel 9
- ❖ **Day 174** - Mark 6:30-56; 2 Samuel 16; Daniel 10:1-21
- ❖ **Day 175** - Mark 7:1-13; 2 Samuel 17; Daniel 11:1-19

❖ **Day 176** - Mark 7:14-37; 2 Samuel 18; Daniel 11:21-45

❖ **Day 177** - Mark 8:1-21; 2 Samuel 19; Daniel 12

❖ **Day 178** - Mark 8:22-9:1; 2 Samuel 20-21; Hosea 1:1-2:1

❖ **Day 179** - Mark 9:2-50; 2 Samuel 22; Hosea 2:2-23

❖ **Day 180** - Mark 10:1-31; 2 Samuel 23; Hosea 3

❖ **Day 181** - Mark 10:32-52; 2 Samuel 24; Hosea 4:1-11a

❖ **Day 182** - Mark 11:1-14; 1 Kings 1; Hosea 4:11b-5:4

❖ **Day 183** - Mark 11:15-33; 1 Kings 2; Hosea 5:5-15

❖ **Day 184** - Mark 12:1-27; 1 Kings 3; Hosea 6:1-7:2

❖ **Day 185** - Mark 12:28-44; 1 Kings 4-5; Hosea 7:3-16

❖ **Day 186** - Mark 13:1-13; 1 Kings 6; Hosea 8

❖ **Day 187** - Mark 13:14-37; 1 Kings 7; Hosea 9:1-16

❖ **Day 188** - Mark 14:1-31; 1 Kings 8; Hosea 9:17-10:15

❖ **Day 189** - Mark 14:32-72; 1 Kings 9; Hosea 11:1-11

❖ **Day 190** - Mark 15:1-20; 1 Kings 10; Hosea 11:12-12:14

❖ **Day 191** - Mark 15:21-47; 1 Kings 11; Hosea 13

❖ **Day 192** - Mark 16; 1 Kings 12:1-31; Hosea 14

❖ **Day 193** - 1 Corinthians 1:1-17; 1 Kings 12:32-13:34; Joel 1

❖ **Day 194** - 1 Corinthians 1:18-31; 1 Kings 14; Joel 2:1-11

❖ **Day 195** - 1 Corinthians 2; 1 Kings 15:1-32; Joel 2:12-32

❖ **Day 196** - 1 Corinthians 3; 1 Kings 15:33-16:34; Joel 3

❖ **Day 197** - 1 Corinthians 4; 1 Kings 17; Amos 1

❖ **Day 198** - 1 Corinthians 5; 1 Kings 18; Amos 2:1-3:2

❖ **Day 199** - 1 Corinthians 6; 1 Kings 19; Amos 3:3-4:3

❖ **Day 200** - 1 Corinthians 7:1-24; 1 Kings 20; Amos 4:4-13

❖ **Day 201** - 1 Corinthians 7:25-40; 1 Kings 21; Amos 5

* **Day 202** - 1 Corinthians 8; 1 Kings 22; Amos 6

* **Day 203** - 1 Corinthians 9; 2 Kings 1-2; Amos 7

* **Day 204** - 1 Corinthians 10; 2 Kings 3; Amos 8

* **Day 205** - 1 Corinthians 11:1-16; 2 Kings 4; Amos 9

* **Day 206** - 1 Corinthians 11:17-34; 2 Kings 5; Obadiah 1

* **Day 207** - 1 Corinthians 12; 2 Kings 6:1-7:2; Jonah 1

* **Day 208** - 1 Corinthians 13; 2 Kings 7:3-20; Jonah 2

* **Day 209** - 1 Corinthians 14:1-25; 2 Kings 8; Jonah 3

* **Day 210** - 1 Corinthians 14:26-40; 2 Kings 9; Jonah 4

* **Day 211** - 1 Corinthians 15:1-34; 2 Kings 10; Micah 1

* **Day 212** - 1 Corinthians 15:35-58; 2 Kings 11; Micah 2

* **Day 213** - 1 Corinthians 16; 2 Kings 12-13; Micah 3

* **Day 214** - 2 Corinthians 1:1-2:4; 2 Kings 14; Micah 4:1-5:1

❖ **Day 215** - 2 Corinthians 2:5-3:18; 2 Kings 15-16; Micah 5:2-15

❖ **Day 216** - 2 Corinthians 4:1-5:10; 2 Kings 17; Micah 6

❖ **Day 217** - 2 Corinthians 5:11-6:13; 2 Kings 18; Micah 7

❖ **Day 218** - 2 Corinthians 6:14-7:16; 2 Kings 19; Nahum 1

❖ **Day 219** - 2 Corinthians 8; 2 Kings 20-21; Nahum 2

❖ **Day 220** - 2 Corinthians 9; 2 Kings 22:1-23:35; Nahum 3

❖ **Day 221** - 2 Corinthians 10; 2 Kings 23:36-24:20; Habakkuk 1

❖ **Day 222** - 2 Corinthians 11; 2 Kings 25; Habakkuk 2

❖ **Day 223** - 2 Corinthians 12; 1 Chronicles 1-2; Habakkuk 3

❖ **Day 224** - 2 Corinthians 13; 1 Chronicles 3-4; Zephaniah 1

❖ **Day 225** - John 1:1-18; 1 Chronicles 5-6; Zephaniah 2

❖ **Day 226** - John 1:19-34; 1 Chronicles 7-8; Zephaniah 3

❖ **Day 227** - John 1:35-51; 1 Chronicles 9; Haggai 1:1-2:23

❖ **Day 228** - John 2; 1 Chronicles 10-11; Zechariah1

❖ **Day 229** - John 3:1-21; 1 Chronicles 12; Zechariah2

❖ **Day 230** - John 3:22-36; 1 Chronicles 13-14; Zechariah3

❖ **Day 231** - John 4:1-26; 1 Chronicles 15:1-16:6; Zechariah4

❖ **Day 232** - John 4:27-42; 1 Chronicles 16:7-43; Zechariah5

❖ **Day 233** - John 4:43-54; 1 Chronicles 17; Zechariah6

❖ **Day 234** - John 5:1-18; 1 Chronicles 18-19; Zechariah7

❖ **Day 235** - John 5:19-47; 1 Chronicles 20:1-22:1; Zechariah8

❖ **Day 236** - John 6:1-21; 1 Chronicles 22:2-23:32; Zechariah9

❖ **Day 237** - John 6:22-59; 1 Chronicles 24; Zechariah10

❖ **Day 238** - John 6:60-71; 1 Chronicles 25-26; Zechariah11

❖ **Day 239** - John 7:1-24; 1 Chronicles 27-28; Zechariah12

❖ **Day 240** - John 7:25-52; 1 Chronicles 29; Zechariah13

- ❖ **Day 241** - John 8:1-20; 2 Chronicles 1:1-2:16; Zechariah 14

- ❖ **Day 242** - John 8:21-47; 2 Chronicles 2:17-5:1; Malachi 1:1-2:9

- ❖ **Day 243** - John 8:48-59; 2 Chronicles 5:2-14; Malachi 2:10-4:7

- ❖ **Day 244** - John 9:1-23; 2 Chronicles 6; Malachi 2:17-3:18

- ❖ **Day 245** - John 9:24-41; 2 Chronicles 7; Malachi 4

- ❖ **Day 246** - John 10:1-21; 2 Chronicles 8; Psalm 73

- ❖ **Day 247** - John 10:22-42; 2 Chronicles 9; Psalm 74

- ❖ **Day 248** - John 11:1-27; 2 Chronicles 10-11; Psalm 75

- ❖ **Day 249** - John 11:28-57; 2 Chronicles 12-13; Psalm 76

- ❖ **Day 250** - John 12:1-26; 2 Chronicles 14-15; Psalm 77

- ❖ **Day 251** - John 12:27-50; 2 Chronicles 16-17; Psalm 78:1-20

- ❖ **Day 252** - John 13:1-20; 2 Chronicles 18; Psalm 78:21-37

❖ **Day 253** - John 13:21-38; 2 Chronicles 19; Psalm 78:38-55

❖ **Day 254** - John 14:1-14; 2 Chronicles 20:1-21:1; Psalm 78:56-72

❖ **Day 255** - John 14:15-31; 2 Chronicles 21:2-22:12; Psalm 79

❖ **Day 256** - John 15:1-16:4; 2 Chronicles 23; Psalm 80

❖ **Day 257** - John 16:4-33; 2 Chronicles 24; Psalm 81

❖ **Day 258** - John 17; 2 Chronicles 25; Psalm 82

❖ **Day 259** - John 18:1-18; 2 Chronicles 26; Psalm 83

❖ **Day 260** - John 18:19-38; 2 Chronicles 27-28; Psalm 84

❖ **Day 261** - John 18:38-19:16; 2 Chronicles 29; Psalm 85

❖ **Day 262** - John 19:16-42; 2 Chronicles 30; Psalm 86

❖ **Day 263** - John 20:1-18; 2 Chronicles 31; Psalm 87

❖ **Day 264** - John 20:19-31; 2 Chronicles 32; Psalm 88

❖ **Day 265** - John 21; 2 Chronicles 33; Psalm 89:1-18

- ❖ **Day 266** - 1 John 1; 2 Chronicles 34; Psalm 89:19-37

- ❖ **Day 267** - 1 John 2; 2 Chronicles 35; Psalm 89:38-52

- ❖ **Day 268** - 1 John 3; 2 Chronicles 36; Psalm 90

- ❖ **Day 269** - 1 John 4; Ezra 1-2; Psalm 91

- ❖ **Day 270** - 1 John 5; Ezra 3-4; Psalm 92

- ❖ **Day 271** - 2 John 1; Ezra 5-6; Psalm 93

- ❖ **Day 272** - 3 John 1; Ezra 7-8; Psalm 94

- ❖ **Day 273** - Jude 1; Ezra 9-10; Psalm 95

- ❖ **Day 274** - Revelation 1; Nehemiah 1-2; Psalm 96

- ❖ **Day 275** - Revelation 2; Nehemiah 3; Psalm 97

- ❖ **Day 276** - Revelation 3; Nehemiah 4; Psalm 98

- ❖ **Day 277** - Revelation 4; Nehemiah 5:1-7:4; Psalm 99

- ❖ **Day 278** - Revelation 5; Nehemiah 7:5-8:12; Psalm 100

❖ **Day 279** - Revelation 6; Nehemiah 8:13-9:37; Psalm 101

❖ **Day 280** - Revelation 7; Nehemiah 9:38-10:39; Psalm 102

❖ **Day 281** - Revelation 8; Nehemiah 11; Psalm 103

❖ **Day 282** - Revelation 9; Nehemiah 12; Psalm 104:1-23

❖ **Day 283** - Revelation 10; Nehemiah 13; Psalm 104:24-35

❖ **Day 284** - Revelation 11; Esther 1; Psalm 105:1-25

❖ **Day 285** - Revelation 12; Esther 2; Psalm 105:26-45

❖ **Day 286** - Revelation 13; Esther 3-4; Psalm 106:1-23

❖ **Day 287** - Revelation 14; Esther 5:1-6:13; Psalm 106:24-48

❖ **Day 288** - Revelation 15; Esther 6:14-8:17; Psalm 107:1-22

❖ **Day 289** - Revelation 16; Esther 9-10; Psalm 107:23-43

❖ **Day 290** - Revelation 17; Isaiah 1-2; Psalm 108

❖ **Day 291** - Revelation 18; Isaiah 3-4; Psalm 109:1-19

- ❖ **Day 292** - Revelation 19; Isaiah 5-6; Psalm 109:20-31
- ❖ **Day 293** - Revelation 20; Isaiah 7-8; Psalm 110
- ❖ **Day 294** - Revelation 21-22; Isaiah 9-10; Psalm 111
- ❖ **Day 295** - 1 Thessalonians 1; Isaiah 11-13; Psalm 112
- ❖ **Day 296** - 1 Thessalonians 2:1-16; Isaiah 14-16; Psalm 113
- ❖ **Day 297** - 1 Thessalonians 2:17-3:13; Isaiah 17-19; Psalm 114
- ❖ **Day 298** - 1 Thessalonians 4; Isaiah 20-22; Psalm 115
- ❖ **Day 299** - 1 Thessalonians 5; Isaiah 23-24; Psalm 116
- ❖ **Day 300** - 2 Thessalonians 1; Isaiah 25-26; Psalm 117
- ❖ **Day 301** - 2 Thessalonians 2; Isaiah 27-28; Psalm 118
- ❖ **Day 302** - 2 Thessalonians 3; Isaiah 29-30; Psalm 119:1-32
- ❖ **Day 303** - 1 Timothy 1; Isaiah 31-33; Psalm 119:33-64
- ❖ **Day 304** - 1 Timothy 2; Isaiah 34-35; Psalm 119:65-96

* **Day 305** - 1 Timothy 3; Isaiah 36-37; Psalm 119:97-120

* **Day 306** - 1 Timothy 4; Isaiah 38-39; Psalm 119:121-144

* **Day 307** - 1 Timothy 5:1-22; Jeremiah 1-2; Psalm 119:145-176

* **Day 308** - 1 Timothy 5:23-6:21; Jeremiah 3-4; Psalm 120

* **Day 309** - 2 Timothy 1; Jeremiah 5-6; Psalm 121

* **Day 310** - 2 Timothy 2; Jeremiah 7-8; Psalm 122

* **Day 311** - 2 Timothy 3; Jeremiah 9-10; Psalm 123

* **Day 312** - 2 Timothy 4; Jeremiah 11-12; Psalm 124

* **Day 313** - Titus 1; Jeremiah 13-14; Psalm 125

* **Day 314** - Titus 2; Jeremiah 15-16; Psalm 126

* **Day 315** - Titus 3; Jeremiah 17-18; Psalm 127

* **Day 316** - Philemon 1:1-25; Jeremiah 19-20; Psalm 128

* **Day 317** - James 1; Jeremiah 21-22; Psalm 129

- ❖ **Day 318** - James 2; Jeremiah 23-24; Psalm 130

- ❖ **Day 319** - James 3; Jeremiah 25-26; Psalm 131

- ❖ **Day 320** - James 4; Jeremiah 27-28; Psalm 132

- ❖ **Day 321** - James 5; Jeremiah 29-30; Psalm 133

- ❖ **Day 322** - 1 Peter 1; Jeremiah 31-32; Psalm 134

- ❖ **Day 323** - 1 Peter 2; Jeremiah 33-34; Psalm 135

- ❖ **Day 324** - 1 Peter 3; Jeremiah 35-36; Psalm 136

- ❖ **Day 325** - 1 Peter 4; Jeremiah 37-38; Psalm 137

- ❖ **Day 326** - 1 Peter 5; Jeremiah 39-40; Psalm 138

- ❖ **Day 327** - 2 Peter 1; Jeremiah 41-42; Psalm 139

- ❖ **Day 328** - 2 Peter 2; Jeremiah 43-44; Psalm 140

- ❖ **Day 329** - 2 Peter 3; Jeremiah 45-46; Psalm 141

- ❖ **Day 330** - Galatians 1; Jeremiah 47-48; Psalm 142

❖ **Day 331** - Galatians 2; Jeremiah 49-50; Psalm 143

❖ **Day 332** - Galatians 3:1-18; Jeremiah 51-52; Psalm 144

❖ **Day 333** - Galatians 3:19-4:20; Lamentations 1-2; Psalm 145

❖ **Day 334** - Galatians 4:21-31; Lamentations 3-4; Psalm 146

❖ **Day 335** - Galatians 5:1-15; Lamentations 5; Psalm 147

❖ **Day 336** - Galatians 5:16-26; Ezekiel 1; Psalm 148

❖ **Day 337** - Galatians 6; Ezekiel 2-3; Psalm 149

❖ **Day 338** - Ephesians 1; Ezekiel 4-5; Psalm 150

❖ **Day 339** - Ephesians 2; Ezekiel 6-7; Isaiah 40

❖ **Day 340** - Ephesians 3; Ezekiel 8-9; Isaiah 41

❖ **Day 341** - Ephesians 4:1-16; Ezekiel 10-11; Isaiah 42

❖ **Day 342** - Ephesians 4:17-32; Ezekiel 12-13; Isaiah 43

❖ **Day 343** - Ephesians 5:1-20; Ezekiel 14-15; Isaiah 44

❖ **Day 344** - Ephesians 5:21-33; Ezekiel 16; Isaiah 45

❖ **Day 345** - Ephesians 6; Ezekiel 17; Isaiah 46

❖ **Day 346** - Philippians 1:1-11; Ezekiel 18; Isaiah 47

❖ **Day 347** - Philippians 1:12-30; Ezekiel 19; Isaiah 48

❖ **Day 348** - Philippians 2:1-11; Ezekiel 20; Isaiah 49

❖ **Day 349** - Philippians 2:12-30; Ezekiel 21-22; Isaiah 50

❖ **Day 350** - Philippians 3; Ezekiel 23; Isaiah 51

❖ **Day 351** - Philippians 4; Ezekiel 24; Isaiah 52

❖ **Day 352** - Colossians 1:1-23; Ezekiel 25-26; Isaiah 53

❖ **Day 353** - Colossians 1:24-2:19; Ezekiel 27-28; Isaiah 54

❖ **Day 354** - Colossians 2:20-3:17; Ezekiel 29-30; Isaiah 55

❖ **Day 355** - Colossians 3:18-4:18; Ezekiel 31-32; Isaiah 56

❖ **Day 356** - Luke 1:1-25; Ezekiel 33; Isaiah 57

❖ **Day 357** - Luke 1:26-56; Ezekiel 34; Isaiah 58

❖ **Day 358** - Luke 1:57-80; Ezekiel 35-36; Isaiah 59

❖ **Day 359** - Luke 2:1-20; Ezekiel 37; Isaiah 60

❖ **Day 360** - Luke 2:21-52; Ezekiel 38-39; Isaiah 61

❖ **Day 361** - Luke 3:1-20; Ezekiel 40-41; Isaiah 62

❖ **Day 362** - Luke 3:21-38; Ezekiel 42-43; Isaiah 63

❖ **Day 363** - Luke 4:1-30; Ezekiel 44-45; Isaiah 64

❖ **Day 364** - Luke 4:31-44; Ezekiel 46-47; Isaiah 65

❖ **Day 365** - Luke 5:1-26; Ezekiel 48; Isaiah 66

❖ **Day 366** - Luke 5:27-39; Genesis 1:1-2:25; Psalm 1 [Day 366]

Made in the USA
Columbia, SC
07 December 2022

72361999R00050